W9-CCF-094

Taking Your Camera to
BRAZIL

Ted Park

STECK-VAUGHN
ELEMENTARY · SECONDARY · ADULT · LIBRARY

A Harcourt Company

www.steck-vaughn.com

Printed and bound in the United States of America
10 9 8 7 6 5 4 3   W 03 02

Photo acknowledgments

Cover ©Eduardo Garcia/FPG International; p.1 ©PhotoDìsc; p.3a ©Julia Waterlow; Eye
Ubiquitous/CORBIS; p.3b ©Telegraph Colour Library/FPG International; p.3c ©PhotoDisc; p.3d ©Corel
Photo Studios; p.5 ©iSwoop/FPG International; p.8 ©Corel Photo Studios; p.9 ©PhotoDisc; pp.10, 11
©Eduardo Garcia/FPG International; p.13 ©Julia Waterlow; Eye Ubiquitous/CORBIS; p.15a ©Corel Photo
Studios; p.15b ©Stephen Simpson/FPG International; p.17 © Jon Spaull/CORBIS; p.19 ©PhotoDisc; p.20
©Corel Photo Studios; p.21 ©Michael Hart/FPG International; p.23 ©Telegraph Colour Library/FPG
International; p.25 ©Renzo Gostili/AP/Wide World Photos; p.27 ©Eduardo Garcia/FPG International;
p.28a ©PhotoDisc; p.28b ©Ed Taylor Studio/FPG International; p.29a Comstock Klips; p.29b, c ©Eduardo
Garcia/FPG International.

All statistics in the Quick Facts section come from *The New York Times Almanac* (1999)
and *The World Almanac* (1999).

Contents

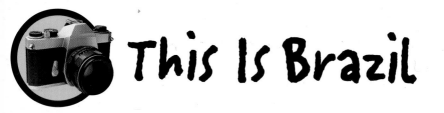# This Is Brazil

Brazil is a huge country in South America. In fact, it is so big that it makes up almost half of South America. Brazil has thick green forests known as rain forests. They are filled with many kinds of plants and animals. Brazil has many rivers and waterfalls. It also has sandy beaches. If you took your camera to Brazil, you could take photographs of many different types of places.

Brazil also has big cities. One of them is São Paulo. São Paulo is the largest city in Brazil. It has many tall buildings. It has wide streets that are filled with cars. It has many people.

This book will show you some of the amazing sights of Brazil. It will also tell you much about the country. By learning about Brazil before you take your camera there, you will enjoy your visit more.

A house built on stilts along a river in the Amazon jungle.

The Place

Brazil is the fifth largest country in the world. It is about the same size as the United States.

The Atlantic Ocean is on the eastern side of Brazil. Brazil's coastline is one of the longest of any country in the world. It is 4,652 miles (7,491 km) long. Most of the people in Brazil live close to this coast. The rest of Brazil borders ten other countries of South America. That shows you just how big Brazil is!

Most of the land in Brazil is low and flat. There are some mountains in the north.

The Amazon River flows through almost half of Brazil. It is the second longest river in the world.

Much of the northern part of the country is covered by the Amazon rain forest. This is the largest rain forest in the world. In a rain forest the trees grow very tall and close together. Some trees in the Amazon rain forest are 200 feet (60 m) tall.

Most of Brazil is warm all year-round. Brazil is cooler in the far south. In fact, it may even snow there in the winter.

Heavy rains fall in the summer, from December through February. Because Brazil is in the Southern Hemisphere, the seasons there are the opposite of those in the United States.

Giant water lilies grow in Brazil's rain forest.

 8

Brazil has about 275 waterfalls. They are very near one another. One of the most beautiful waterfalls in the world is in Brazil. It is called Iguaçu Falls.

Iguaçu Falls, which is near the border with Argentina

Rio de Janeiro

Rio de Janeiro is one of the best-known cities in the world. In English this name means "River of January."

Rio is famous for its sandy beaches. Many people come to Rio from all over the world to sun themselves on these beaches. Its most popular beach is Copacabana.

Copacabana Beach

Sugar Loaf Mountain rises above Rio's beautiful harbor.

Rio is on a bay on the Atlantic Ocean. At the entrance to the bay is a tall, pointed mountain on one side of it. This mountain is called Sugar Loaf Mountain. Nearby is another mountain. It is called Corcovado Mountain. On top of Corcovado Mountain is a large statue of Jesus.

If you took your camera to the top of either of these mountains, you could take many interesting photographs. You could photograph Rio's beautiful harbor and beaches. You could also take photographs of the mountains near the city.

11 📷

Places to Visit

The first capital of Brazil was the city of Salvador. It has more than 100 old churches. Many of them are decorated with gold.

The city of Manaus is in the northwestern part of Brazil. In the late 1800s, it was the only place in the world where people could get rubber. Today it is a major trading center for the area around the Amazon River. Manaus has a famous opera house. It also has a popular garden filled with many different types of plants and flowers.

Brasília became the new capital of Brazil in 1960. This city was built on an empty plain in the center of Brazil. Brasília has many big buildings. Some of them are used by the people who run the government.

Government offices in Brasília

13 📷

 # The People

About 170 million people live in Brazil. They are a mixture of many peoples. Native peoples were living in Brazil when the Portuguese came in 1500. At one time there were about five million of these people. Now there are only about 200,000.

Many black people live in Brazil. Some of them have ancestors who came to Brazil from Africa hundreds of years ago. The Portuguese had brought them there and forced the people to work for them.

By the 1800s, more than 500,000 people from Portugal had moved to Brazil. This is why Brazilians speak Portuguese. In every other country in South America, the people speak Spanish. Later, many Italians and Germans came to Brazil. Many people from Japan came, too. Today, Brazilians are a mix of natives, Portuguese, Africans, and many other peoples.

A man
dressed in
traditional
clothes

A Brazilian businesswoman

# Life in Brazil

Most Brazilians live in cities. Many of them came from the countryside to find work there. In the big cities some people with little money live in houses made of wood or brick with a tin roof. Many of them do not have electricity or running water. People who have more money may live in houses that have gardens and swimming pools. In Brazil there is a big gap between the poor and the rich.

Family life is very important to Brazilians. It is not unusual for grandparents, parents, and children to live together in the same house.

About $4\frac{1}{2}$ million people are born in Brazil every year. Brazil has the fifth largest population in the world.

New apartment buildings and smaller homes are often side by side in Brazilian cities.

Government and Religion

Brazil has been a republic since 1889. This means that Brazilians elect a president, or leader of the country. A president is elected every five years.

Brazil's government has three branches. The president and the president's helpers are the executive branch. They make sure that laws are obeyed. The Senate and the Chamber of Deputies is the branch that makes the laws. The judicial branch, made up of judges, makes sure the laws are fair.

Most Brazilians are Roman Catholic. They believe and follow the teachings of the Catholic church.

Almost every town in Brazil has a Catholic church.

 18

 # Earning a Living

Brazil has many natural resources. A natural resource is something that comes from nature and is useful to people. Some of Brazil's natural resources are lead, iron, gold, and bauxite. Bauxite is a mineral used to make aluminum. Brazil also has plenty of gas, coal, and oil. Workers mine, or dig up, all these things.

A man in Belem selling from a street stand

Sugarcane being harvested in Brazil

Many Brazilians work in factories. Making cars is important in Brazil. There are also plenty of jobs for people who build houses.

In the south there are large farms. Coffee is grown on many of them. Brazil is the world's largest grower of both coffee and sugarcane. It is also the world's largest supplier of oranges, lemons, and other fruits.

 School and Sports

More than half of all Brazilians are under age 20. Children are supposed to go to school from the ages of 7 to 14. After 14, some go on to high school and then college. However, many children don't go to school. They stay at home to help with the work. Also, in many parts of the country, there are no schools.

Soccer is the most popular sport in Brazil. It is sometimes known by its Portuguese name, *futebol*. People in Brazil like to watch soccer games. Maracaña Stadium in Rio de Janeiro is the largest soccer stadium in the world. It can hold 200,000 people. Brazil's soccer stars and teams are known all over the world. Brazilians also like car racing and horse racing.

Most Brazilians enjoy soccer games.

 22

Food and Holidays

In much of Brazil the favorite meal is black beans and rice. Sometimes the dish is served with a spicy sauce. Some people also add bits of meat to it. When meat is added, the meal is called *feijoada*. Meat is particularly popular in the southwest, where there are great cattle ranches. Fish is popular along the Amazon River and on Brazil's coasts. Fruit is also served at most meals.

Carnival is a lively time all over Brazil. This festival takes place in February or March. In Rio, the festival is a big one. Floats and parades fill the streets. Prizes are given to the float with the best decoration. Some 20,000 people take part in the parade. Many of them dress up in very fancy costumes. People sing and dance.

A dancer at Carnival

The Future

Brazil has many natural resources. When they are exported, or sent, to other countries, that brings money into the country. But mining these resources can hurt the land and poison the air and water.

People are cutting down more and more trees in the Amazon rain forest. They use the land to grow crops and build houses. Because of this, plants and animals in the rain forest are dying out.

Brazilians want to solve these problems. They have a Portuguese expression. It is "*dar um jeito.*" In English this means "to find an answer to a problem." As Brazil faces a new century, it is a good and useful expression. The people of Brazil know they must find a way to save the Amazon rain forest for future Brazilians. They have set aside large areas in the rain forest as wildlife parks. Thay are also teaching their children how to protect the land.

An oil platform off the coast of Brazil

 26

Quick Facts About
BRAZIL

Capital
Brasília

Borders
French Guiana, Suriname, Guyana,
Uruguay, Venezuela, Colombia,
Peru, Bolivia, Paraguay, and
Argentina

Area
3,286,475 square miles
(8,511,965 sq km)

Population
169.8 million

Largest cities
Sao Paulo (9,842,059 people);
Rio de Janeiro (5,547,033 people);
Belo Horizonte (2,060,804 people)

Chief crops
coffee, soybeans, wheat, rice, beef

Natural resources
bauxite, gold, iron ore

Longest river
Amazon, at 903 miles (1,500 km)

Flag of Brazil

◀ **Coastline**
4,652 miles (7,491 km)

Monetary unit
real

Literacy rate
83 percent of Brazilians can
read and write

Major industries
textiles, shoes, chemicals

29

Glossary

Brasília (bruh-ZIL-yuh) The present-day capital of Brazil

Carnival (KAR-nuh-vol) A lively Brazilian festival that is held every year during February or March

Copacabana (ko-puh-kuh-BAH-nuh) A popular beach in the city of Rio de Janiero

executive branch (ig-ZEK-yout-iv) The branch of the government that makes sure that laws are obeyed

feijoada (FAYZHUH-wah-dah) A popular Brazilian dish made of black beans, rice, and pieces of meat that is served with a spicy sauce

Iguaçu Falls (ee-gwuh-SOO) A waterfall in southern Brazil

judicial branch (joo-DISH-uhl) The branch of the government that makes sure that laws are fair

Manaus (mah-NOWSH) A city in the northwestern part of Brazil that once had supplied all of the world's rubber

natural resource Something that comes from nature and is useful to people